Celtic Mythology

A Guide to Celtic History, Gods, and Goddesses

Jordan Parr

Table of Contents

Introduction 1

Chapter One: Celtic Gods and Goddesses 3

Chapter Two: The Monsters and Heroes of Celtic Mythology 9

Chapter Three: How the Celts Worshipped Their Gods 15

Chapter Four: Celtic Traditions 20

Chapter Five: The Great Stories of Celtic Myth 29

Chapter Six: What Remains of Celtic Mythology in the Modern World? 36

Final Words 48

Introduction

Before one begins to study and understand the mythology of the people known as *Celts*, they first have to understand who the members of this ancient community were. The Celts were not a centrally located people, nor were they one single culture. They were a collection of tribes and chiefdoms controlled by a hierarchy of barbarian leadership. In this sense, *barbarian* represents a group of people not belonging to any of the major Western civilizations: The Romans, Greeks, or Christians. The original Celts were an Iron Age group called *Druids*, and they were known for initiating the holidays we now know as Halloween and Christmas. They were a powerful religious sect and a warring collection of tribes. Their central location was what is now modern-day Britain—England specifically. There are no Druids left today, but their ancestry remains embedded in the modern-day British Isles.

Celts inhabited the land from as far west as Ireland and as far east as the Black Sea along the edge of Ukraine. They were made up of individual clans, each with their own dialect of the Celtic tongue, and they were once the largest group in Europe. Today, there are several regions that still speak the native Celtic languages: Ireland, Scotland, Wales, Cornwall, and the Isle of Mann. However, Celtic blood remains in all these locations, as well as in Northern France and the Basque Country of Spain.

Like all great cultures, the Celts had their own sense of spirituality and religion. Their beliefs were tied deeply to nature and the land they inhabited. They are a people indigenous to the parts of the continent on which they roamed. They were both seafaring and farming people. They were warriors and priestesses. They were powerful and subjugated, and they brought every bit of their traditions into their lives even as they were forced to adapt to the ruling classes. No matter the situation, the Celts were sly and insistent to remain Celts. Even to this day, one can hear the beat of Irish step dancing or recite a prayer to St. Brigid in a Roman Catholic church, and without realizing it, they're continuing on with the spiritual and mythological practices of their ancestors. They are an ancient and indelible people and, like in so many other cultures, their mythology tells the story of who they were, who they are, and who they will continue to be.

Chapter One: Celtic Gods and Goddesses

To better understand the mythology of the Celts, one first must dive in deeper and look at who they worshipped and why they worshipped them. There were hundreds of Celtic gods, big and little, but there were a few select ones that were the most well-known. They're listed here in alphabetical order, not necessarily in order of importance to the Celtic peoples.

The Celts believed that it was at the first light of day that all mysteries were revealed. As the sun lit the Earth, the stones and rough patches were made clear, the fresh dew on the grass glittered in the light, and the questions one had about the decisions they should make were made clear at that very moment between the deepest darkness and the first rising of the sun. It was in these moments, when the Celts believed their gods were most likely to speak. At dawn, the greatness of Celtic spirituality became known.

Celtic spirituality and mythology have inspired and touched so much of life around the world today. From music to literary theory and language, the Celts have spread their influence, sensibilities, and culture through nearly every area of life on the planet. From Spain and Austria, to Ireland and Scotland, to Wales and France, the Celts never dissolved as some ancient civilizations did. Instead, they simply evolved to become an even more prominent thread in our modern-day tapestry.

Alator: A hungry mother might seek this god to provide a bountiful harvest for her family. It is unclear if he was originally worshipped by the Celts or if he was an adaptation of the Roman god Mars, but his key attributes were kindness and compassion. He was looked to when the Celts felt neglected or were in need of encouragement. A new parent might pray to Alator every morning for the first year of a child's life, knowing that this was the most precarious time in any human's existence.

Albiorix: Another god frequently associated with the Roman god Mars was Albiorix. He was considered the "king of the world" and was known for his fiery and sudden temper. He could be called upon to both save the Celts from sure disaster and punish them with a raging storm from the bitter cold waves of the North Sea. He was both young and old, a symbol of what was and what will be, and a nod to the Alpha and Omega of Greek mythology as well. It is also said that he may have been influenced by the Greeks as well. He was easily adapted into something similar to the early Christian belief of a one *true* god as he is considered *king* of the world.

Belenus: This god spanned the continent, from the Mediterranean region to the British Isles. Belenus has many variations, from the Italian-sounding *Belinos* to the French *Beltaine*. As a surname, it is still commonly used in the Celtic region of northern Spain and is represented in the very common Spanish surnames Belus and Velez. When the Romans came upon the god Belenus, they worshipped him as they did their god Apollo because they saw the similar attributes of healing and health. Belenus was prayed to by the sick to treat anything from a minor cold to a major illness. It was said that approaching Belenus was always a successful endeavor. He was always willing and eager to support those in need. However, in the rest of the Celtic world, the god most often associated with healing was Lenus.

Borvo: Borvo was only worshipped in northern France. He was associated with healing springs, and whenever water was a blessing to one in need, Borvo was praised.

Brigantia: Brigantia was the most powerful of the goddesses in the region that is now known as the British Isles. She was also associated with healing waters, rivers, and water cults. Entire religious offshoots formed around this powerful goddess. The word *brigantine* comes from Brigantia's name and describes a large, two-masted sailing ship associated with power and beauty.

Brigit: Brigit remains one of the most popular Celtic goddesses of today. She evolved from being the goddess of fire, fertility, new life, cattle, and harvest into one of the most popular Roman Catholic Irish saints. As a saint, her intercession is relied upon to bring about protection and to look after smiths and domestic animals. She is also the patroness of poetry, something the most ancient Celtic goddess was also associated with. It is unclear if Brigid the saint was a real person. Some scholars argue that she existed first as a Druid priestess who lived in a monastery devoted to the goddess Brigit, but that she later converted to Christianity and lived as a nun. The myth recounts Brigid converting the whole of the Druid monastery to a Christian one.

Cerwiden: Cerwiden is a shape-shifting goddess who was believed to be the inspiration that created poetry across the Celtic world. If one had a song in their heart and or verse on their tongue, they were said to be inspired by Cerwiden. She kept a cauldron of wisdom and fear—respect for elders—in her home and could see the future in it.

Cernunnos: This was the god of fertility, strength, and wealth. He was regularly associated with two-horned animals, like the bull and ram. These animals were also used as his symbols and in Latin he was called *Dis Pater,* which means "of the Father" and is a meaning and term that is closely associated with modern day Christianity.

Epona: This goddess was one of the only gods that had no association with any Roman god. Frequently, the Romans would bring their gods to the Celts, and vice versa. The two cultures would adapt their beliefs and mix them to suit their needs. However, Epona the goddess of fertility, was adapted by the Romans without any change. They loved her as she was and built a temple for her. She was associated with oxen, donkeys, and horses and was said to accompany souls when searching for their final resting place, whether it be heaven or hell.

Esus: Esus was a woodcutter god and was heavily associated with human sacrifice. This is another Gallic (northern French) god, and he was primarily worshipped in that region.

Latobias: Latobias was a Celtic god worshipped in the Alpine region of Austria. He was rightly associated with mountains and skies as well as worshipped for his beauty that was displayed in these elements.

Lugh: Here was a god associated with craftsmanship and the sun. He was said to actually be the embodiment of the sun, and that his presence was manifested in the heat of solar rays. He was also known as Lamfhada. Cú Chulainn, the famous demigod of Irish folklore, is said to be the manifestation of Lugh. He was most popular in Ulster, but is one of the most infamous of the Celtic gods. He took on more than one shape and image and was known for his battle frenzy called *ríastrad*. Many monsters, demons, and other folklore have developed their own imagery and characters based on Cú Chulainn.

Manopus: Manopus was associated with music and poetry. He was closely associated with other Roman gods and was popular with both groups, the Celts and the Romans. He was considered a fun-loving god who bestowed joy on his people.

Medb/Maeve: Medb was also known as Maeve, which is a popular Irish and Scottish Celtic name even to this day. She was the goddess of Connacht and Leinster (the name of the Irish parliament) and was known to have many husbands. She's considered, by some Celtic scholars, as having been one of the original Celtic deities, but not much else is known about her today.

Morrigan: Morrigan is the Celtic goddess of war and battle, and she manifested herself as a crow or a raven. When these creatures were seen at the time of battle, they were considered as a sign that Morrigan was among the warriors, defending her people. Today, Celtic lore states that a crow or a raven is a sign of Morrigan, but she's now revealing an omen or a warning to be watchful, as danger could be near if one is foolish. In Celtic mythology, the hero Cu Chulainn rejected her in marriage, and when he died, Morrigan revealed herself to him as a crow.

Nehalennia and Nemausicae: These are two very similar deities. They are both goddesses of fertility and mothers. But Nehalennia is also the goddess of those at sea, and Nemausicae is another Celtic goddess of healing.

Nerthus: Nerthus is worth noting as one of the rare Germanic and Celtic goddesses. Her attributes are unknown.

Nuada: Nuada was considered one of the most powerful and popular of the Celtic gods. He was worshipped the length of the Celtic world. He was known for healing and wielded an invincible sword that sliced his opponents in half. Legend states that when he lost his hand in battle, he lost his ability to serve as king. However, his brother gifted him a silver, replacement hand, but he was later killed by the Celtic god of death, Balor.

Chapter Two: The Monsters and Heroes of Celtic Mythology

Sometimes the heroes of Celtic lore mirror the monsters. They often possess the same traits, but whether they are heroes or monsters depends on what side of the story the protagonist is standing on. Some heroes could be villains to those they're attacking but to others they could be great protectors. It often depended on the clan being saved over the clan being attacked. However, no matter where you look for these evil do-gooders, you'll find a lot of information within the Celtic myths. They are numerous. There were even a few real-life individuals whose reputations were so incredible throughout the Celtic nations that their lives were turned into myth, and we don't know much about which parts are true. But we still hold them in myth so we can meet them—the ancestors of the Celtic peoples today. Here are a few of the most popular.

The Monsters

Abhartach: Abhartach is considered the most terrifying of the Irish monsters. He appears in several other Celtic myths as well. He's considered the Irish vampire and an early version of the *walking dead*. He drinks the blood of his victims and is known, in some Irish texts, to have consulted both saints and Druid priests to find his victims. He's feared and tales of him are told throughout Ireland to this day. He's said to wander the earth seeking fresh blood. Some scholars of Celtic mythology and history believe that it was from the Abhartach that Bran Stoker, an Irish native himself, derived the story of Dracula and not from the true history of Vlad Tepec of Romania. This is a debatable suggestion. However, what is not debatable is the fact that the tale of the Abhartach is as old as the Celts themselves.

Balor the Evil Eye: In Celtic mythology, there are many demon leaders. Clans called on them to do their bidding, and priests fought them in order to do the bidding of the Christian God. One of the most famous leaders of the demon hoards was Balor the Evil Eye. He was said to be able to summon thousands of demons to attack his enemies. He was a giant monster with a huge eye that was made powerful when he was discovered spying on his father's druids one night. A foul vapor entered his open eye, thereby granting him the ability to cause death to anyone who met his gaze. To this day, rural parts of Ireland and Scotland are careful about the "Evil Eye" and what dangers lurk for those who look into it. Sometimes an amulet is even worn to ward it off. Other times a simple prayer will do. Either way, the story of the "Evil Eye" came from Balor and his fateful encounter with the druids at worship that day.

The Banshee: Of all the monsters in Celtic mythology, none are more infamous than the Banshee, who comes at night and wails at the window of the dying. It was believed among ancient Celtic peoples that the Banshee, a ghostly female figure adorned in flowing white rags and sometimes a skeleton face, would float outside the window of a dying person's house. She could be young or old, beautiful or terrifying to look at. Either way, her appearance meant something ominous for whoever heard or saw her. She would begin her mournful wail at a low, quiet whisper, and it would gradually increase to a screeching high-pitched cry, reaching its highest volume just before the person passed away. The banshee is also sometimes used to threaten children into behaving to avoid the risk of the banshee coming after them. Additionally, sometimes small children are said to be "crying like a banshee" when their pitch is especially loud, disconcerting, or high-pitched. A banshee can also be associated with a wild or unkempt woman.

The Oillipheist: The Oillipheist is a dragon monster from Celtic lore. It was said to haunt the deepest and darkest lakes of Ireland, Scotland, and Wales. It could be seen swooping and shooting fire from its mouth, the reflection of its flames visible against the waves. The famed Loch Ness Monster was believed to have been an Oillipheist. In Celtic mythology, chieftains and warriors regularly fought this dragon in heavy battles. In nearly every major battle tale of Celtic mythology, there is one Oillipheist that is being fought. Sometimes the Oillipheist is a symbol for a personal struggle in modern life, like an addiction or a chronic illness that is difficult to treat.

Faeries: These creatures could be either evil or good. They were believed to inhabit the thick forests of Western Europe and would regularly shape-shift into various forms, tricking people into doing their bidding. Their trickery would often result in the death, or the eternal enslavement of the people caught under their spell. Faeries usually have wings and create hypnotic, melodic tunes, enticing people deep into the forest where they will become lost and can never find their way out. Some faeries, however, are considered kind and protective. Of all the monsters in Celtic mythology, the faerie is one of the most famous. Seelie faeries are commonly depicted as good faeries who abide by a law, while Unseelie faeries are seen as harmful and lawless.

The Changeling: This monster is more common in Scottish and Welsh mythology than in any other, but they are nonetheless infamous. A changeling is a deformed, or sickly, faerie infant that is discovered crying in the forest. A human adult will become concerned about it and take it into their own home, where the Changeling will snatch any human infants in the residence and trade places with them. The Changeling takes on the human's form and returns to the faeries, where they grow strong and contribute to the faerie stock. The human baby's soul is fed to the Devil.

Kelpies: Another well-known water monster is the Kelpies. These creatures inhabit the *lochs* (lakes) in Celtic lands, taking on the shape of water horses. They will look kind and innocent, drawing the human to them. Once the human is close enough, the Kelpie will snatch them and take them deep into the water with it, sealing the person's certain doom.

Selkies: Selkies are a version of Celtic mermaids. They can be male or female, and they are said to be very attractive. They live in the sea and will come on land to find a partner or a human of romantic interest. However, they cannot live on the land if they have their skin, which they shed when they hide by the water. If a human can find their skin and bury it, they get to keep their Selkie partner for life. However, if they don't find their skin and still try to keep their Selkie love interest captive, the Selkie can become violent. Most often in Celtic mythology, they simply remained on land until they found their skin again, and no matter how deep their human relationships, they would return to the sea once they did.

The Blue Men of the Minch: These monsters look like humans but are smaller and have blue skin. They live in *the Minch*, which is the waterway between mainland Scotland and the Outer Hebrides islands. They speak in rhyme, and the Chieftain will capture ships and demand that the captain complete the poem they've presented him with. If he can't, they'll swallow his ship whole. They are also believed to be responsible for all storms out at sea.

The Bodach: This creature is similar to the boogeyman of English and American lore, but he differs in temperament across Celtic lands. In some cultures, he would be described as harmless—a man who played silly tricks on children. However, to the Scottish and Welsh, he was said to kidnap children who misbehaved.

The Leprechaun: The Leprechaun is probably the most well-known of the Celtic creatures. He is both a good and bad creature. He can be seen dancing and playing a flute. He guarded a pot of gold at the end of the rainbow, but Leprechauns were mischievous creatures that would send a man to his death before giving up his gold. If a human discovered the Leprechaun's hiding place at the end of a rainbow, they were granted the pot of gold. However, if he spotted the Leprechauns, or *Little Men*, without seeing the pot of gold, he ended up as a slave to the Leprechauns forever.

The Gancanagh: Similar to faeries and Selkies, these monsters could seduce both men and women with an alluring scent. It was said to be so seductive that any human who encountered the smell couldn't turn away from it. The Gancanagh would then put a spell on the person they'd seduced, and the person would die shortly thereafter.

Heroes

While it's already been stated that there was sometimes little separation between the monsters and heroes of Celtic mythology, one of the great differences was that a hero existed to protect his or her people. While their methods of battle and revenge might be equal in ferocity and violence, a hero of Celtic myth would always look after the poor, respect the gods of the land, and usually die so that others might live.

The heroic tradition of Celtic mythology began in what is known as *the Ulster Cycle*. Here, such gods and heroes as Cu Chulainn began their reign and legends.

The earliest written record of the tradition of the Celtic hero belongs to the seventh century, but there can be no doubt that it had already lived through several centuries of oral existence.

Besides the heroes already mentioned here in the book, Cu Chulainn, Fionn MacCumhaill, Brigid, and Patrick, there was also King Arthur. While many associate him purely with English literature, that is not accurate as he was of Celtic origin. The famous king, his Knights of the Round Table and his wizard, Merlin, are all of deep Celtic mythological origins. Their history was an oral one long before it was written down. And while there is obviously no record of a real King Arthur, there has long been speculation that he might have been based on a real person, just as many Celtic myths utilized the lives and names of real people to tell fictional stories. The first books written about Arthur date back to the 15th century, but there have been many more authors since then. There have been several movies and musical tracks created with Arthur and his knights at the center.

Chapter Three: How the Celts Worshipped Their Gods

The Iron Age Celts were an incredibly spiritual people. They had hundreds of gods and goddesses, known and unknown, so many that this book is an introduction to scratching the surface. Hundreds of texts have been written about the Celts and how they worshipped. Archeologists, historians, and other scholars have routinely stated that all we know about the Celts and their spirituality is only what's on the surface. They are an ancient people with centuries of evolving culture all around them. Even after centuries, we haven't found an end to their traditions.

Sacrifices

Every Halloween, children all over the world trick or treat, dressing up in often scary costumes to knock on the doors of strangers and ask for candy. This practice comes directly from one of the Celts most famous and important religious festivals—Samhain. During what is the most important holiday on the Celtic calendar, the Celts would burn the first fruits of the fall harvest, dress up in the costumes of the things they feared most, and celebrate the oncoming darkness. Many rituals and legends have grown out of this holiday, but what is important about it, from a scholarly perspective, is why and how the Celts worshipped during this holiday.

The Celtic spiritual beliefs were deeply linked to nature and natural phenomenon. They worshipped not only the gods who created the world in which they lived but also the land itself. During Samhain, both the light (the moon) and the darkness (the night) are honored for their place and importance in the everyday lives of the Celtic people. It was believed that on this night, evil spirits roamed the earth, but if one was a trustworthy and good person, evil could not touch them. The darkness would not be able to overcome them, and they would prevail to see the dawn.

It was also a holiday of great thanks, where the Celtic people would burn large hay bales and a sampling of the crops they had worked so hard to cultivate during the springtime. They didn't do this because they were wasteful or unappreciative of their bounty; they believed the gods they worshipped wanted this sacrifice from them. Sacrifice was a pillar of Celtic worship.

When Celts worshipped, they sought the guidance of their priests, the Druids. There is not much known about the Druids, but what we do know is that they were the most important people, aside from chieftains, in Celtic culture. Even the chieftains needed the spiritual guidance of their priests.

When illness, famine, or war would sweep a Celtic land, the Druids were called on to protect the people. They would often retreat to the highest point in an area and pray for a predetermined number of days. Seeking the highest point was very important in ancient Celtic existence, and it is surmised that this is one of the reasons for the building of high cairns (tombs) or mounds. It was atop these places the priests would pray for the dead.

In order to stave off further disaster, the Celts would first resort to sacrifice. These sacrifices could be as small as offering one's god a place at the dinner table and leaving a heaping plate of food for them. It could also mean leaving food or gifts on the edge of the front porch, so that the gods seeking praise would find the gifts in the night. If the gift was gone in the morning, it was believed the god was pleased and would spare the family or sick person. However, if it was left behind, the god was angry, and the suffering would continue until the proper sacrifice had finally been made.

The worse the suffering was, the greater the sacrifice it would require. Sometimes this would instigate a soldier in battle tossing his best sword into the deepest lake. He would offer his greatest protection to the god who he believed could save him. Sometimes an entire army would need to release their weaponry to the loch. Archeologists found more than 150 objects of war in and around Llyn Cerrig Bach. It is believed that these weapons were sacrificed to gods of protection when men at battle feared losing their lives.

The Celts would sacrifice animals as well, just as they did with crops. If a herd was especially fruitful one year, the farmer might sacrifice a cow or pig to the god whom he believed blessed his family. He might also sacrifice livestock if things were not going so well for him. If a Celt felt as though their personal sacrifices were not yielding anything, they would seek the assistance of a Druid, who would likely charge a hefty price for their services. Their rituals could last days and might involve seeking out the highest mountain or peak. But when the work was done, and the sacrifice was complete, the Druids would suggest a certain number of days the person should wait for a response—or reaction—from the god. If things improved, the god was said to be pleased. If things didn't, the sacrifices became more costly.

It has long been known that Celts regularly participated in human sacrifice. For centuries, the suggestions of Celtic human sacrifice were considered Roman propaganda. Not many scholars believed it to be reality, but then in the early 1980s the body of a Druid priest was discovered in England. He was called "the Lindow Man," and he was clearly staged for an elaborate sacrifice.

When archeologists found him, they discovered that his beard had been trimmed and his nails had been neatly manicured. His head had been bashed in, he'd been strangled, and his throat had been cut to facilitate the highest amount of blood loss possible. All of this happened about the same time that the Celts began to lose their culture and power to the invading Romans. It's believed that the local tribe was trying to thwart another Roman attack, and so they offered this important human sacrifice to the only gods they believed could protect them. They seemed to have a premonition of how much destruction was coming their way, so they took matters into their own hands.

We know now that it wasn't Roman propaganda that suggested the Celts regularly participated in human sacrifice. They actually believed the eating of human flesh was an important energizer before battle. They also believed the gods delighted in the murder of human beings, so it was not at all rare for a Celtic clan to murder their enemies, their prisoners, and even innocent women and children to appease an angry god or seek the assistance they needed in battle. Some evidence suggests that the Druids were often willing to offer themselves up as this sacrifice if their countrymen needed them. In the case of the Lindow Man, it's suggested that he may have willingly offered himself to the gods.

Cannibalism

Cannibalism was another form of worship for the Celts. They didn't just sacrifice humans; they also ate them. While it was once believed to be a rare occurrence, we have evidence that proves it wasn't uncommon at all. Eating human flesh was a regular part of Celtic worship, and it was one of the reasons the ancient Celts were feared by their enemies. They would even display this tradition during battle to strike fear in the hearts of those who sought to cause them harm.

But these were not the only ways that Celts showed their love and respect for the gods they worshipped. They also offered valuable objects to them. Any object of importance to a person, a household, or a clan could be offered to the gods for their protection and blessing. From food to an iron sword, gifts could be offered in exchange for help. It is believed that this is possibly where the idea of gift-giving came from in the early Halloween and Christmas holidays. Before they became a Christian tradition, they were Celtic-pagan traditions, and gift-giving to the gods was a major part of Celtic spirituality.

Though it was once believed to be pure anti-Celt propaganda, we now know that the Celts worshipped their gods through cannibalism as much as they did through the sacrifice of objects—and animals—and they celebrated in a way that reflected their devotion to nature.

Chapter Four: Celtic Traditions

Music

Nothing is more recognizable in Celtic life than music. As soon as one hears the bagpipes or an Irish fiddle, they know they're hearing something of Celtic roots. From the very beginning of its society, Celtic culture has embraced and used music as a means of communication, worship, and connection across the whole of the Celtic world. There are specific rules and parameters surrounding Celtic music, and it is one of the most widely known, accepted, and practiced of the Celtic traditions. It spans all of the Celtic nations—ancient and modern.

Irish traditional music, similar to most traditional music, is characterized by slow-moving change, which usually occurs along accepted principles. Songs and tunes believed to be ancient in origin are revered. However, it is difficult or even impossible to know the age of most tunes due to their tremendous variation across Ireland and through the years; some generalization is possible—for example, only modern songs are written in English, with few exceptions, the rest are penned in Irish. Most of the oldest songs, tunes, and methods are rural in origin, though more modern songs and tunes often come from larger cities and towns.

The purest form of the Celtic musical tradition is a vocal-only method called *sean nós*, which simply means "in the old style." It is considered the ultimate expression of Celtic music. Each Celtic culture has its own version of this style, even if they refer to it by a different name. Every line utilizes a different melody, and it's sound is very distinctive, causing some scholars to draw a connection between it and ancient Middle Eastern musical styles. The melodies always have a haunting quality and are sung in some form of Gaelic. They're instantly recognizable. When listeners hear them, they know it's Celtic music they're hearing. These tunes are sung at weddings, funerals, religious celebrations, and other important events in Celtic culture. Usually, only one person is allowed to sing the melodies, but sometimes a duet is performed. There is no instrumentation involved. The unique instrumental combination is another aspect of Celtic music altogether. In traditional instrumental Celtic music, the violin and guitar are most recognizable, while the tin whistle was introduced only after the Industrial Revolution and is not a true Celtic instrument. It was simply an instrument of convenience that was popularized because it traveled easily in the pockets of those carrying it to and from musical performances.

Scottish and Welsh music has also played a part in this very important aspect of Celtic tradition and culture. Most notably, the Scottish are known for their bagpipes, but these are also not traditionally Celtic. They came from other parts of Europe and migrated to Scotland several centuries earlier. They were quickly integrated into Scottish battle songs and were utilized in a similar way that drums were used in other European armies. They relayed a battle plan or the change of plans to soldiers marching in the field. They were also used to inspire and encourage the weary and wounded. Today, we see the bagpipes being used in Scottish music both in Scotland and abroad for important ceremonies, parades, celebrations, and in popular Celtic music. There are still some clans that are associated with the bagpipe, as they were some of the first ones to use this instrument, essentially creating this tradition.

As with music, dance is another deeply important aspect of Celtic life today just as it has been for centuries. Jigs, reels, strathspeys, and waltzes are all group dances that are regularly a part of Celtic celebrations.

Spirituality

Celtic spirituality is unique in its approach to religion and faith, even today. It springs from the pagan and druid aspects of Celtic history but also the Christian influence that has made its mark on Celtic life since the fourth century. There are several important aspects to Celtic spirituality, which are all active parts of the Celtic tradition.

Thresholds

Both the ancient Celts, and the Celts of today, readily accept the value and importance of thresholds. These are the spaces between light and dark, dusk and dawn, old and new, and the edge of change. It's in these places of transition Celtic tradition teaches us that something vitally important is happening. It's just at the break of dawn when Celtic tradition says mysteries are revealed—the stones on our pathway, the flowers in bloom, the rain that falls. It's believed that if one asks for guidance in life, it's at the break of dawn when it will likely come, right at the threshold of time. It's also believed that a person's greatest possibility exists at the moment of change.

Dream

From the days of the druid priests, Celts have believed that dreams hold interpretations of the past, present, and future. Just as in modern psychology, it's believed that things and actions of dreams represent the subconscious mind. This idea is not far from the ancient Celtic belief that dreams send a message to the dreamer. Dream interpretation is a Celtic tradition that spans generations, and when utilizing this Celtic tradition, dreamers are urged to evaluate their dreams for messages. Famous figures in Celtic mythology and religion have frequently relied on their dreams to help them solve problems or find a way out of trouble.

Blessing the Day

Not only are blessings a common way of approaching anything new in Celtic tradition, but the blessing is also a way to approach anything. Naturally, there are blessings for births, deaths, weddings, and great moments of celebration, but these are not the blessings that are referenced here. The most important blessings of Celtic tradition are the "blessings of the moment." Everyday life—the little things—are considered the most important aspects of life. Waking up receives a blessing. Taking a walk receives a blessing. Lying down to rest, opening a book, pouring a cup of tea, washing the dishes, etc. all receive blessings. Why? Because any moment that proves the progression and continuity of life is a gift and deserves a blessing. People are encouraged to savor every moment and not to simply ask for blessings from whatever spiritual practice they adhere to, but to actively bless the moment themselves. The ancient Celts believed that every human being had the ability to give a supernatural blessing to other people and things. So, the idea of blessing the day is meant as a lesson: we have the power to change our attitudes and our outlooks on life. This comes from the Celtic tradition of living *moment by moment*. Because no one knows how many moments they will have in life, Celtic tradition encourages us to count them all and to bless them with intention and purpose.

I Arise Today

I arise today
Through the strength of heaven:
Light of sun,
Radiance of moon,
Splendor of fire,
Speed of lightning,
Swiftness of wind,
Depth of sea,
Stability of earth
Firmness of rock.

— Kuno Meyer, *Selections from Ancient Irish Poetry*

The Solemnity of Fire

Fire is a sacred element in the Celtic world. It is treated with the utmost of respect across the Celtic lands. Whether it was used in the treatment of dead wood, crops, or religious ceremonies, fire was looked upon as both a nourisher of heat and warmth and a deadly monster if handled incorrectly. For this reason, it was often the druid priests alone who performed any religious tradition utilizing fire. There were very clear rules and regulations surrounding the usage of fire, and a house set ablaze was said to be cleansed of demons or disease. If one caught on fire, in very ancient Celtic times, it was believed that this was the will of the gods, even if it was seemingly an accident. In modern Celtic society, even stepping on the embers of a fire is said to bring very bad luck to the head of the household. Fire is the symbol of the son, and the son is the highest symbol of the ultimate deity.

Friendships of the Soul

In Celtic tradition, it's important to have a *soul friendship* or a kind of mentorship and connection with another person that goes deeper than usual friendship. It's the kind of relationship where honesty and integrity are paramount. Both parties make regular attempts at bettering the life of the other and give guidance and hope to their friend. It's a platonic friendship and is not restrictive in gender. What is important is that it feels miraculous, like something that has come straight from the heavens, and it's a friendship that will last a lifetime. In many cases, one's soul friend knows their counterpart better than they know themselves. One of the main ideas behind such a friendship is that, as humans, it's often very difficult for us to be objective about the problems in our own lives. It's also difficult for us to be honest about our talents and gifts. Here's where a soul friend steps in. This is a person who knows, instinctively, what is good for us, even when we're at a loss. They reach out and offer that wisdom to us and expect us to do it for them in turn.

The Celtic Calendar

Another prominent tradition in Celtic culture is the lunar calendar. Like many ancient cultures, the Celts had their own lunar calendar and followed the moon, sun, and stars—and the rest of the natural world—as a guide to order their days and nights. Their festivals were all centered around the movement of these objects within the universe.

The Celtic world once consisted almost exclusively of farming communities, and they regulated their lives by the time spent between equinoxes and solstices. The more light a season had, the greater the growing potential. The less light a season had, the more time spent indoors. This tradition dates back to, at least, the Neolithic age. Today's calendar reflects its connection to the old one through being separated by new moons, full moons, quarter moons, and the equinoxes that still tell us which seasons are just on the edge of the horizon. As with the ancient Celts before us, we still measure our lives in days and nights today.

In Gaelic, the term for month is *mios* and the term for year is *bliadhna*. The latter refers to the "separation of time" within a certain cycle of moons.

The Gaelic year began in November following the festival of Samhain, which later evolved into Halloween); and it ushers in the first of the new seasons: winter. The cold was considered necessary to cleanse the land and prepare it for the new, bountiful year ahead. In Gaelic, it is rendered *Geamhrahd*, coming from an early Celtic term for cold, which in turn comes from an even more ancient linguistic source for *stiff and rigid*, describing the frosty ground. Within Geamhradh, there are three 'months' of *Dubhlachd, Faoilleach,* and *Gearran,* meaning—the Dark Days, the Wolf Month, and the Cutting or Gelding Month, respectively.

Just as the cold had value in the Celtic world, so did heat and fire, and they were utilized as an aspect of healing and cleansing. Flames from candles, the bonfires of Samhain, the twinkling of the stars, etc. were all seen as a moment of renewal within the darkness. The darkest months of the year were referred to as the "Wolf Months," because they were often hungry months. They were hungry for light and warmth and longer days, and the people experiencing these months, and the loss of crops within them, were also often experiencing physical hunger as well. These were also the months when the wolves came down from the hills and the mountains to scavenge for food. If an animal had to be castrated, it was done during that time so that it could heal better. If other animals were to be slaughtered, the slaughtering was done at that time if possible, so as to protect from the greatest amount of disease. Even in ancient times, when little to nothing was known about bacteria, the Celts still had an idea that the warmer it was outside, the higher likelihood that one would not heal from a wound. So, any surgical procedures were considered to have the best chance of ending well if they were done in January and February.

November was the equivalent of January to these ancient peoples. For them, the year began with Samhain. All three winter months were separated by their value to the farming world, and their names reflected that same usage. December was *Dubhlachd,* which means "the dark days." January through February were together *Faoilleach,* "the Wolf Months." And March was *Gearran,* "the cutting or gelding month."

Because spring always brings harsh rain and storms, it was associated with the Roman god, Mars, even for the Celts. They called spring *Màrt. T-Earrach* was high spring and represented all that was good about life beginning anew. It was a time of rebirth and rejuvenation and trying new things. It was, in short, another physical threshold that drew people into a deep spiritual connection. It was also referred to as "the pudding month," because this was the season when the leftover stores from the long, dark winter were mixed together into a pudding and eaten in a great end-of-the-cold festival.

Summer, the season of warmth, long sunny days, and the growth of the new life that came forth in spring, was called *Samhradh*. This Gaelic word references the heat of the sun on our face, our backs, and across the Celtic lands. June specifically is referred to as the "youngest month," and it is called *t-Ogmhìos*. It was in this month wishes were made—and many promises too. It's when many Celtic weddings were held and when the gods were called upon to bless a new endeavor.

The hottest month of the year in Scotland is July, and it is the main holiday month correspondingly—it is also the month with the least chores on the farm. In Gaelic it is *t-Luchar*, simply the "warm month." The first great harvest festivals began in the balmy days of August, which is called *Lùnasdal*. The God Lùgh was a hero god of skill, artistry, and war and seems to have had pan-Celtic appeal. The name derives from root words for sun, shining bright, and lightning; and it may simply correspond to the long blue-sky days of August or to the lightning storms that accompany the humidity. Either way, he was a popular figure in Celtic mythology, and the bread feasts were almost certainly dedicated to him. In old Scots the *Lammas* (loaf-mass) fair took place in August, and there is likely a linguistic connection.

The very last month of the Celtic year was September, also known as *Sultain*, a month when the cattle would be fattened—and the livestock and land prepared for the winter. Autumn in Gaelic was called *Foghar*, which comes from the root word for hospitality. In these times, it was important to focus on community and welcoming one another.

Old rifts were mended, and people were forgiven for their mistakes. It was a great time of reconciliation. Forgiveness was the center focus of *Foghar*, and those seeking asylum also found it in the places they were once expelled from. We see a reflection of this today in the inviting smells and images of autumn, in the warm colors of the leaves, the focus on comfort foods, and family celebrations around the world. This has deep roots in the Celtic tradition of yesteryear.

It would have been impossible to function in an ancient Celtic world without the guidance of the moon, the sun, and the stars. The Celtic calendar, still very much accessible today, was an excellent resource that became a rich tradition in its own right.

Chapter Five: The Great Stories of Celtic Myth

Celtic mythology is broken down into four different cycles: The Mythological Cycle that comes largely from Ireland and is associated with deities and supernatural beings. The Fenian Cycle that revolves around hunting; these include both Scottish and Irish tales. The Ultonian/Ulster Cycle that tells the stories of the Ulaidh lands. And finally, the Kings Cycle, which is a collection of stories about the Celtic kings—some of whom were real kings doing impossible things.

From the Mythological Cycle

The story of the Children of Lir (Fionnuala, Fiachra, Aodh, and Conn)

The four children of King Lir are transformed by his new wife—a strange, red-headed beauty who shows up to his home unannounced and bewitches him. The children know something is up, but they encourage each other to be brave and strong like their father and to trust that Aofie was going to love them after all. One day, she tricked them down to the river, where she turned them into ducks using strange words they'd never heard before. She cursed them to remain as ducks until they heard the sounds of a very particular bell. The curse was to last nine hundred years. Only one sorcerer could make the sound and break the spell, but he could not be summoned. He would not allow himself to be beckoned. He would only come as he pleased, and by chance. The children called out for King Lir when he came to search for them. When he discovered they had all been turned into ducks, he cursed his wife, Aoife, and called her a vile queen before sending her away.

The children continued to love their father and encouraged him to be strong and brave, as he'd always taught them to be. They said they'd never stop loving each other or him, even though they remained in this curse for 300 years. They left the water only after their father, the king, had died. At his death, it is the Irish belief that he became a star. The children flew to an island called InishGlora, where they believed the sorcerer to live. There, they found the holy man, Mochaomhóg, and he healed them and turned them back into children again. After which, they flew into the sky and became one with the stars and their father again.

The Seven Trials of the Fianna

This is the story of legendary Fionn MacCumhaill, son of Cumhaill and the leader of a fierce band of Irish fighters and hunters called "the Fianna." They defended Ireland from invaders, monsters, demons, and anything else that threatened it. There are many stories about Fionn and the Fianna. In one famous story, Fionn meets his wife in the forest while she is disguised as a deer. Before his very eyes, she turned into a beautiful woman, and they married immediately. After their son was born, Fionn's wife turned back into a deer, left him, and kept his son from him for years. Eventually, the son and father reunited.

The Giant Causeway

This is another famous story about this Irish, mythical warrior. Legend has it that Fionn and the Fianna created the Causeway, so that they could use it as a bridge to Scotland where they would fight the giant Benandonner. However, when Fionn arrived, he discovered a sleeping Benandonner and knew that he was outmatched. He was, in fact, a massive giant. Fionn fled back over the Causeway while Benandonner slept.

Back in Ireland, Fionn's wife dressed him up like a baby, and when the Scottish monster came over to Ireland to fight Fionn, he found only a baby and his mother at their house. Fionn's wife begged the giant not to wake the "baby," and seeing that the baby was so large, Benandonner convinced himself that the father must be all that much larger. So, he fled back to Scotland.

> "Truth in our hearts,
> Strength in our arms,
> Honesty in our speech."
>
> *—The Rule of the Fianna*

As entertaining as these stories are, the most famous story of Fionn MacCumhaill is the story of the Seven Trials of the Fianna. In this tale, Fionn sets out to be surrounded by only the fiercest warriors in all of Ireland. So, he puts the Fianna through a set of extremely difficult tests. He discovers the Salmon of Wisdom—the vision regarding which tests to use—by sitting down beside a river and sucking his thumb. It is there that the ideas come to him.

The men were to first be able to recite poetry and fall in love. They had to be romantic at heart in order to be true warriors. They also had to be able to think critically and love literature. Wielding a heavy sword was not enough. Fionn decided they would fight the following trials in groups of three.

The First Trial of the Fianna: In this trial the warriors had to leap over an object as tall as themselves to show vigor.

The Second Trial of the Fianna: In this second trial they had to crawl under a height as low as their knees without touching it to show flexibility.

The Third Trial of the Fianna: In the third trial warriors were called upon to run as fast as they could until they stepped on a large thorn that pierced their feet to show speed.

The Fourth Trial of the Fianna: The fourth trial demanded that they pull the thorn out without losing stride to show agility.

The Fifth Trial of the Fianna: In the fifth trial the Fianna had to recall—from memory and without mistake—the twelve collections of poetry passed down by the bardic file and the druids. One mistake and they would immediately be disqualified.

The Sixth Trial of the Fianna: The sixth trial was the most difficult and it was here that many Fianna were said to begin to shake, but showing fear was not as serious of a problem as losing. In this trial the warrior was buried up to their belt inside a hole. The other Fianna were given spears and stabbed at the buried warrior while the only thing the buried Fianna was given to protect himself with was a stick. He had to fend off the entire band with only that one stick.

The Seventh Trial of the Fianna: If one completed this entire stream of battles, and lived to tell the tale, they were commanded to take a wife for love, not dowry, and to live out the rest of their days in passion and peace with her.

By far, this is the most popular of the tales and many versions of it can be found throughout Celtic literature.

The Ulster/Ultonian Cycle

The Birth of Cú Chulainn

No doubt, the most famous of Celtic warriors was Cú Chulainn, who created and solidified the stories of Celtic Mythology. In his birth story, a group of fifty maidens from Ulster went missing, and though the warriors of Fergus had set out to find them, they were never successful. Generations passed, and one day, the area was being overrun by a group of fifty crows who mocked the farmers. Townspeople came out and threw stones and food at them, threatening them and begging them to leave, but all they would do is beckon them deeper into the countryside. Eventually, the warriors fell upon a cave, where a beautiful maiden had given birth to a child. This child was eventually given to the king, where it grew strong and brilliant, and eventually sacrificed his own life for Ireland in battle. His original name was Setana, but he was later called Cú Chulainn.

The Hound of Cullan

When Setana was big enough, he was sent to live in the Court of Connor with the other warrior boys. However, he was smaller than the others, and they mocked him as he approached them. This infuriated Setana, and he single-handedly fought all the boys in the school, defeating each one without struggle. From this infamous fight, he was thenceforth called Cú Chulainn, as he is known throughout Celtic myth.

When Cú Chulainn grew into young adulthood, King Connor and his nobles set off to a banquet at a nearby castle. Cú Chulainn was in the midst of a game of hurley—which can best be explained as a mix between baseball, cricket, and field hockey. The nobles saw that he was engaged and left him there. They promised to wait up for him to arrive. However, they drank and feasted until they fell asleep, leaving Cú Chulainn alone to deal with the mighty hound of Cullan. It had a ferocious bark and a bloodcurdling growl that would strike terror throughout the entire Celtic lands when it was heard. The men were awakened by it when Cú Chulainn approached, and these mighty warriors were terrified for the young man. They knew he would never survive an attack by the mighty hound of Cullan. However, what the men discovered when they shone the light of their lamps onto the front yard of Cullan's castle, was Cú Chulainn standing mighty and the dog dead on the ground. As it turned out, Cú Chulainn had grabbed the ferocious beast by the throat and instantly killed it. Once again, the boy once known as Setana had made a name for himself as Ulster's mightiest warrior.

Cú Chulainn, spoken widely of in this book, is one of the most important figures in Celtic myth. It's very important, if one wants to get a good grasp of what the ancient Celts felt about any given subject, to explore their stories as much as possible. For it is inside the stories of a people, that one finds the realities of their struggles, their fights for freedom and equality, and their history. It might be hidden deep in the stories of faeries and giants, but the truth stands in the midst of the tales, and nowhere is this more evident than in the great stories that sprung from Celtic Mythology and, most especially, the story of Cú Chulainn.

The Cycle of Kings

The final cycle of Celtic Mythology is the Cycle of the Kings. These stories were written in the eleventh and twelfth centuries by monks who told the imagined stories of the real-life kings of Ireland. They had eclectic names like King Cormac mac Airt, Niall of the Nine Hostages, Conn of the Hundred Battles, Brian Boru, and Boruma.

Each of their tales tell of the rise, struggle, triumph, and death of the kings. Like the rest of Celtic literature, the stories do not leave out the bad parts. Celtic heroes are not always good, never perfect, and sometimes fail. Still, they are loved for the lessons they have taught Celtic peoples for centuries about never giving up, about focusing on your dreams, and about living life for passion and love. Many of these kings were kings in name only, and their myth was so embellished that their real lives resembled their fictional lives very little. In fact, there is much debate as to whether many of them even existed as they were noted in Celtic mythology. The only genuine king of Ireland was Brian Boruma, and he was best known for having defeated the invading Viking warriors at the Battle of Clontarf in 1014. From his name comes the most populous surname in all of Ireland, and in the Irish diaspora: O'Brien. From this alone we can see how important the stories of Celtic myth are to Ireland and beyond.

    The Irish were not the only ones to lay claim to great Celtic stories, but they are the most famous and beloved of the storytellers. In Scotland and Wales, some of the same stories have been adapted and changed from Irish-centric to another version. However, the characters and stories still remain.

Chapter Six: What Remains of Celtic Mythology in the Modern World?

There is hardly a place in the Western World where one can go and not see the influence of the Celts on the modern world. One can see the influence of the Celts from the Basque country of Spain, with its tradition of pilgrimage, to the highest places to find enlightenment, to the deep hollers of Appalachia where a form of old Irish mixed with American English is spoken today. In Northern France, their artifacts and imagery remain. In Ireland, Scotland, and Wales their dialects are still flourishing. From the music to the literature and spiritual practices, like Wicca and neo-paganism, the influence of Celtic mythology and culture is still very much alive today.

The Language and Literature of the Celtic Tradition

From the stories of Cú Chulainn and the druids, to the short stories of James Joyce and Robert Burns, the Celtic people have long shared their history through tale and verse. Even with the many dialects, the Celtic lands spoke in a universally understandable tongue. The language of the Celts is important in understanding Celtic mythology because language is the expression of the people.

The modern living Celtic dialects are Breton, Irish, Scottish Gaelic, and Welsh, with Cornish and Manx recently seeing a revival. Welsh is the official language of Wales, and Irish is the official language of Ireland. Both Welsh and Breton are descended from the Celtic languages of northern France, or Brittony; Scottish and Irish are descended from Middle Irish.

Celtic Language Influence on English

In the United States, Canada, Australia, New Zealand, Jamaica, the Virgin Islands—and anywhere else that both English and a Celtic language was spoken fluently for a hundred years or more—Celtic versions of common English words have developed. For example, in the American South, it's not uncommon in the Appalachian region, where the Scots-Irish, Irish, and Welsh immigrants mostly settled, to hear someone talk about planning a "shindig" or party. Shindig comes from the Scottish Gaelic word *shinty*, which was the name of a game played in a manner like hockey. The player would kick their leg up, or to the side, in order to strike the ball or pitch it to another player. From this came the moniker "shindig" when talking about a party where people might be dancing to Irish or Scottish music. Since Appalachian music has its roots in mostly Celtic and African music, it also has many connections and utilizes many words that are rooted in Gaelic.

The word "malarkey" is another example of how the Irish and Scottish tongues slipped easily into the mouths of their diaspora. Malarky means silliness, fanciful talk, or untrue words. It comes from an Irish surname that is pronounced the same. It's not readily known exactly where the word comes from, but it is wholly Irish-American in its usage and is popular today. It began circulation around the time of the Great Migration of the 1890s when the Irish fled Ireland in droves for the New York Harbor and a better life in the United States.

Additionally, there are whole sections of Canada that still carry a Celtic lilt in their accent. For example, parts of Nova Scotia still retain aspects of their ancestors' Irish and Scottish accents. When heard, they often sound as though they never left these countries at all.

The Influence of Celtic Music on Music Around the World

While it was mentioned in an earlier section of this book that Celtic music is an important Celtic tradition, so are the musical traditions that developed from the Celtic diaspora. American country music, especially Bluegrass, is very similar to Scottish, Welsh, and Irish music. However, it has also influenced rock music, Jazz, and musicals. With the building of the railroad across the United States, the Irish and newly freed, African American slaves would often learn each other's musical traditions. Something new and different came from the combination. The African banjo, the Industrial Revolution's contribution to old Celtic music, the tin whistle, and a new form of Afro-Celtic music was born.

Bluegrass is America's Celtic music. It often uses direct Celtic words and references, and it has its roots alongside the music of immigrants who came to the Appalachian region of the United States from Ireland, Scotland, Wales, and England. It is easy to hear the reels and jigs of Celtic Europe in the ditties and tunes being played in a West Virginia coal town's Christmas celebration. The Scots, Welsh, Irish, and even English settlers—who trekked over the Blue Ridge Mountains through Virginia, West Virginia, Kentucky, Tennessee, and North Carolina—brought their lively instrumental ballads and drinking songs to America. From there, a distinctive root of Country music was formed and then named for the famous turf that grows native to Kentucky and Tennessee. Other forms of Celtic-American music formed soon after, like Texas Swing, the Okie melodies of Woody Guthrie, and the mournful Blues songs of Ledbelly. The combination of African American and Celtic music created a new brand of song that would spread out into several other genres, making it one of the most popular, and important, aspects of Celtic influence in the modern world.

Tying the Knot

The idea of "tying the knot" in weddings comes from the Celtic tradition of handfasting. This is when two hands are tied together to symbolize the binding of two hearts, two minds, and two lives. The ancient Celts would use thick strands of wheat or vines, but this eventually turned onto rope and even satin threads. Today, a handfasting ceremony can be performed in the traditional Celtic manner or with modern sensibilities and rituals included.

The ceremony goes back to about 7000 BC and is still very popular today. It was more of a betrothal than it was an actual wedding ceremony, which was much more elaborate, even in ancient Celtic times. Once the couple's hands were fastened together, they would wait one year to see if they were still suitable to each other and to their families. If they remained in love, they'd go back to the priest and ask to be formally married. If the priest, or anyone else objected, they'd be refused formal marriage—and the bonds were broken permanently.

The Claddagh Ring

Though deeply connected to Irish culture, especially in the Irish-American community of the United States, the Claddagh ring was not first created by the Celts. However, it was adopted and embellished by them, so it became part of the larger Celtic culture. It is used in both Irish and Scottish heritage.

The Claddagh ring was first developed by the Romans and was used not only in weddings and familial contracts but also in daily life. If someone was making a legal promise to another, even in business, including slavery that was extremely common throughout the Roman Empire, a ring with two interlaced hands would be worn. Soon, the lasting symbol became connected to marriages and betrothals. A prospective husband would give the father of the woman he wished to marry, a *fede* ring, which means "hands joined in faith" in Latin. If accepted by the father, this ring would be saved for the wedding, put on the bride during the ceremony, and would signify the lifelong bond between husband and wife. The same ring could be used to show betrothal if a woman was too young or not ready to marry, her future husband would also have her wear a *fede* ring to show her loyalty to him. In addition, the *fede* ring did not only express the bride's dedication and promise, but it showed the groom's as well. If he was to cheat on his future wife while she was bearing his ring, there would be grave consequences.

The Romans brought this popular ring and custom to the Celtic lands in the fourth century. It quickly caught on; however, the Irish and Scottish added their own touches to the ring. As early as the 1700s, English jewelry designers were adding a heart in the center of the Claddagh ring. This became a distinctive Celtic look. In the United States, the beautiful design became increasingly popular, and with the Great Migration to America in the late 1890s, the Claddagh ring was quickly associated with Irish- and Scottish-American culture.

Today, this ancient symbol of faith, love, and friendship can be found in just about any jewelry store and at every Celtic festival or market across the country and around the world. When one sees a Claddagh ring, it's clear that their Celtic ancestors are not far behind. There are several ways to wear the ring and below are just a few.

A Claddagh ring was worn with the intention of conveying the wearer's relationship status:

- On the right hand with the point of the heart toward the fingertips means the wearer is single and might be looking for love.

- On the right hand with the point of the heart toward the wrist means the wearer is in a relationship, someone has captured their heart.

- On the left ring finger with the point of the heart toward the fingertips means the wearer is engaged.

- On the left ring finger with the point of the heart toward the wrist means the wearer is married.

The Tin Whistle and the Bagpipes

Though the tin whistle and the bagpipes were mentioned earlier in the discussion about Celtic musical influences, it's important to note the evolution of these instruments over time, and their extensive and iconic reach into present Celtic life. Whether in one of the original Celtic lands, or in the Celtic diaspora sound the world, when one hears the tin whistle, they immediately connect it to Celtic music.

The tin whistle came directly from Celtic England and was developed at the height of the Industrial Revolution in Europe by designer Robert Clark in the nineteenth century. However, almost all cultures have some sort of fipple flute that emits a high-pitched sound and can be easily stored and played anywhere. There are even instances of Neanderthals employing instruments like the modern-day tin whistle. The tin whistle was used in Victorian parlor music and was considered a children's toy. It is suspected that the player was offered a penny for a tune, and this is where the name comes from.

Today, the tin whistle is an important aspect of Irish and Welsh music. There have always been whistles associated with Celtic music, but they have lost their popularity in place of the convenience and desired sound of the tin whistle. This indelible instrument is one more aspect of the wide and lasting influence of the ancient Celts on our modern world.

The bagpipes are immediately recognizable as Scottish. They, like the tin whistle, were not created by Celts. They were brought to the Celts from other parts of Europe. However, they were quickly adopted and integrated into all aspects of Scottish music. From reels to marches, the bagpipes can be heard. When immigrants sailed to America, Australia, or Canada, they brought the pipes with them. Many Irish and Scottish immigrants in the United States entered law enforcement, as it was one of the few professions they were allowed to practice. When a Scottish police officer dies in the line of duty, even now, the bagpipes are used during the procession to their grave and the funeral itself. It no longer matters whether or not the officer had any connection to the Celtic tradition from which the bagpipes come. It is commonplace to hear the Scottish bagpipes played at the memorial service of a law enforcement officer without much exception.

Highland Games

The Highland Games are held in Scotland, and now all around the world, in the spring and summer. Traditional games like the caber throw, the weight throw, mass band competitions, and the parade of the clans—when various Scottish, Welsh, and Irish clans are called out from the crowd and march together—are celebrated and played throughout the world. These are ancient sports, dating back as far as the history of the Celtic people. Their descendants meet to revel in their Celtic heritage together. The Highland games have even influenced other world competitions, like the Olympic track and field competition.

St. Patrick's Day

Nothing is more Irish than St. Patrick's Day. While not as popular in Ireland as it is in the Irish diaspora around the world, like the United States and Canada, St. Patrick's Day is celebrated with great joy and pride. The revered saint of Ireland was not even Irish. As noted in the Irish heroes' section, St. Patrick was English and actually a *slave* of the Irish. However, he served them well over years, and even after he was freed and returned to England, he went back to Ireland and continued to love and support the Irish people. He is credited with bringing Christianity to Ireland, and there is historical evidence that he was most definitely part of the movement away from traditional pagan Celtic beliefs. However, much of what we know about him is either unclear or simply untrue. Whether or not he chased snakes out of Ireland, wrestled with demons and druids, or walked to the top of a mountain and was assumed to find heaven in death, is all very debatable, but there is no debate that to be Celtic is to consider the impact of St. Patrick.

Nowadays, green is associated with all things Irish, specifically Irish Catholicism, and St. Patrick. So, on St. Patrick's Day green is worn for good luck, corned beef and cabbage is eaten, and Irish music and dance is often performed. So ingrained has Irish culture become in the United States that even people who are not of Celtic descent will celebrate this day. Celtic influence reaches beyond one day and one event. It even spans popular culture, with numerous movies and cartoons about Leprechauns and little people—directly arching back to the celebration of St. Patrick's Day.

Celtic Foods

Much of traditional, American Southern food is influenced by foods from Celtic lands. Mixed with food coming from enslaved African people in the Americas, modern Celtic food has distinctive connections to Scotland, Ireland, Wales, and parts of England. Though some of the food items now have different names, they are descended from the Celtic people of the past. It was the Irish and Scottish immigrants who brought the food traditions to much of the South. Biscuits in America and Canada are not the same as biscuits in Ireland or the British Isles, but they still have the same name. French fries, though they are named after France, we know they really came from the idea of "chips" eaten in Celtic countries, and fishsticks are the fried fish that is typical of Irish and British culture. Many of the traditional foods that Americans and Canadians eat today, and the tea they drink, comes from their Celtic ancestors.

The dish of corned beef and cabbage is probably an Americanization of the Irish bacon and cabbage dish, spurred into life by immigrants. As the Irish moved into large cities like Boston and New York, they settled adjacent to other immigrant groups. The Irish might have settled next to a nice Jewish neighborhood and bought meat from their butchery—not the pork meat they were used to, but a cured beef cut equally amenable to being boiled and stewed. This meat was cured as a preservative and could be kept for a long time, as well as being adapted. While keeping kosher was not something the Irish were concerned with, the meat was good for stewing and long cooking, a style of cooking that the Irish were more accustomed to, given that their meat was likely toughened by work beforehand and stewing helped to tenderize it again.

The Tradition of Irish Pewter

The usage of pewter goes back nearly a thousand years in the Celtic lands. At first, it was used only by the very wealthy. From it came goblets, candlesticks, plates, and bowls. Eventually, however, even the everyday citizens of Celtic countries began using pewter because of its durability and growing affordability. Since the Bronze Age, pewter has been linked to Celtic culture, myth, and experience. Celtic knots and cables are engraved pewters of all kinds, hearkening back to the ancestral lands of Ireland, Scotland, and Wales.

Cables

Celtic cables, though associated with their namesake, are not old at all. They didn't come from ancient Ireland or Wales. Instead, they came from the late nineteenth century from a tiny group of islands off the coast of Ireland called the Aran Islands, As well as the ornately designed sweaters known as Aran-cabled sweaters. The main source of income on the island is fishing, and in the 1890s, the Guernsey jumper was improved upon by locals who didn't have the same fine, expensive wool that others did. They created their own heavy, wool sweaters, with complicated cabled designs. They mirror some of the carved cabling in ancient Celtic stones, stone wear, and jewelry. Some scholars have speculated that, perhaps, these cables once had meaning, but by the time they were being knitted and crocheted into thick wool, they no longer carried any messages. The only purpose was to keep warm and look good doing so. Today, Irish, Scottish, and Welsh wool is famous for its quality. Additionally, the Celtic tradition of knitting and crocheting are also some of the most popular hobbies in the world. The highest quality yarn and knitwear designs come from Celtic lands.

Step Dancing

Both the Irish and the Scottish step dancing tradition is still very popular. They have their origins in the reels of Scotland in the late eighteenth century, but they may go even further back to the jigs of the ancient Celts. Viking raids destroyed most books and writings dating back to the fourth century, but there is ample evidence to suggest that the Celts, from Ireland to northern France and Spain, were dancing the jig.

It is believed that what we know as step dancing today actually originated in Scotland, though it is often referred to as "Irish step dancing." In reality, it is heavily practiced and taught in both countries and is extremely popular in the Celtic-rich regions around the world as well. While this form of dance has always been a part of Irish culture, it wasn't until the birth of the dance and musical *Riverdance* that people around the world became enthralled with it. It was considered a watershed moment in Irish or Celtic step dancing, and the sport was revived again with thousands of step dancing schools springing up around the globe to teach the ancient practice. An artform that had nearly been forgotten, or at least was no longer popular, had suddenly become easily recognizable even in non-Celtic households.

Once thought to be connected to Celtic religious festivals and celebrations, the dances are now performed mostly in cultural celebrations. There are national and international competitions for the sport, and one does not need to be of Celtic origin to compete or become an expert. Dancers are required to keep their upper bodies completely still, while kicking their feet. The intricate movements have meaning and purpose, and no matter where this dance is performed, there is an immediate connection to the ancient artists who invented it.

Wishes Upon a Star

Walt Disney, famous Irish American and designer of the Disney empire, famously encouraged children everywhere to "wish upon a star" so their dreams would come true. This concept, however, was not new when Disney produced the movie *Pinocchio* in 1940. This idea that loved ones become stars after death is an ancient Celtic belief. We see this in the story of "The Children of Lir" in which the children are turned into ducks and taken away from their beloved father, King Lir.

However, when the curse they endure at the hands of their evil stepmother is reversed by a druid holy man, and they do finally meet up with him again, he has already passed on. Instead of joining him on Earth, they join him in the heavens, where he is blinking brightly, punctuating the darkness with his guiding light for them.

This story highlights the strong belief that spawned in ancient Celtic myth and is still a bedtime story told to children today. As the story goes, when a loved one—who has been a good person in life and has those left on Earth who love them—dies, they become a star and light the path for the ones they left behind. In a world where death was an everyday occurrence, and it was not uncommon for mothers to die in childbirth, it became a very convenient and comforting way of giving reassurance to those still living in the fragility of the world. But it was never said that evildoers became stars. They were cursed to wander the barren, Irish countryside, looking for their lost souls—the origins of the Jack-o-Lantern—or to suffer eternal pain. Today, the idea of our loved ones calling our attention to the sky every night comforts us still. When you hear that Disney tune, you can safely imagine that the composer, if not Disney himself, had heard this beloved myth about the afterlife more than once in his own life.

Final Words

Dating back to the Bronze Age, the Celts are a varied and formidable group. They spanned almost the entire European continent and ruled over many regions. Though more than one conqueror tried to erase their presence, they have continued to prevail. Their ancient tongue helped develop many modern languages, and their cultural identity has morphed and evolved to create the Irish, Scottish, Welsh, Cornish, Britons, and more. Even northern Spain and remote places in Austria were not immune to the influences of the people who worshiped at the command and guidance of druid priests. Everywhere one looks in the Western world, they can see the remnants of St. Patrick's Day parades, Highland games, Bluegrass music, Irish Step Dancing, Bagpipes, Gaelic surnames, and the stories and fairytales that dot children's libraries around the world. While many a civilization has come and gone, the Celts have come, stayed, and thrived despite war, hardship, Vikings, the English, famines, and centuries of struggles and triumphs. Who will the Celts be in a few hundred more years? That is not a question we can answer in this book, but we can acknowledge that they will continue to make their mark, and we know they have left us an incredible history to study for another millennia.

This book has covered only the very edge of Celtic mythology and history. In fact, archeologists and historians still have much to learn about who the Celts were, what place the druids really had in Celtic society, and how many nations today have been influenced by the Celts of the past. If you are interested in reading more about this incredible culture, you are in luck, because they have left behind a world of knowledge, music, literature, culinary delights, and spiritual beliefs to guide you through your discovery.

The unity of the Celts was one of culture rather than of race. Those people who the Greeks and Romans knew as Celts no doubt were sprung from various ethnic origins, but in the view of external observers, they had sufficient shared features—language, social and political institutions, and general way of life—to mark them as a recognizably distinct nation.

www.ingramcontent.com/pod-product-compliance
Lightning Source LLC
LaVergne TN
LVHW021740060526
838200LV00052B/3385